SCIENCE COOKERY
THROUGH

Food Energy

Peter Mellett
Jane Rossiter

FRANKLIN WATTS

New York • London • Toronto • Sydney

© Franklin Watts 1992

Franklin Watts, Inc.
95 Madison Avenue
New York, NY 10016

Library of Congress Cataloging-in-Publication Data

Mellett. P. (Peter). 1946-
  Food energy / Peter Mellett. Jane Rossiter.
    p.   cm. — (Science through cookery).
  Includes index.
  Summary: Examines a variety of common foods, the nutrients they
contain, and what happens to them in the body during digestion.
  ISBN 0-531-14247-7
  1. Cookery—Juvenile literature. 2. Food—Juvenile literature.
3. Energy metabolism—Juvenile literature. [1. Food. 2. Cookery.
3. Metabolism.] I. Rossiter, Jane. II. Title. III. Series.
TX652.5.M359   1993
613.2—dc20   92–11238
                                                CIP   AC

Senior editor: Hazel Poole
Series editor: Jane Walker
Designer: Ann Samuel
Illustrator: Annabel Milne
Photographer: Michael Stannard
Consultant: Margaret Whalley

The publisher would like to thank
the following children for their
participation in the photography of
this book: Jack Brownrigg, Tom
Brownrigg, Caroline Rossiter,
Alexander Rossiter, Greta
Smith-Williams and Corinne
Smith-Williams.

Typeset by Spectrum, London
Printed in Singapore

Contents

Introduction

Science Through Cookery is a new, simple and fun approach to learning about science. In each book you will not only read about science, but you will also have first-hand experience of real science. By linking science topics with simple cooking recipes, you can learn about science and at the same time create some delicious recipes. Science is fun when you finish up eating the results of your work!

About this book

Food Energy looks at the different kinds of food that you eat. We find out what these foods contain, and what happens to them inside your body. **Food Energy** explains digestion, and examines the differences between food from plants and food from animals. It also tells you which foods you need to eat to stay healthy.

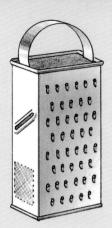

Food Energy explains important scientific principles with the help of clearly labeled diagrams and illustrations. The recipes offer a practical opportunity to gain a better understanding of the science you have just read about.

Each recipe has been carefully selected and written so that the cooking can be done with a minimum amount of adult supervision. Where the help of an adult is needed, for example when boiling a pot of water, this is clearly indicated.

The ingredients and equipment you will need are listed at the beginning of each recipe. They are easily obtainable and no special equipment is required. The step-by-step format of the recipes is easy to follow. Each step is illustrated with a photograph.

At the end of the book you will find a page of Further things to do. These are fun experiments and activities which are linked to many of the science concepts discussed in the book. A glossary of terms and an index are provided at the end of the book.

Your body needs food

Think of all the different kinds of food that you can eat – pizza, yogurt, lettuce, fish, butter, oranges. The list is almost endless. Food contains substances that help you to move about and do work, and to grow and stay healthy.

A car needs energy from its gasoline to travel down the road. You use energy from some of your food to run, walk, climb, and even to sleep. The more work you do, the more energy your body needs from food.

Climbing a mountain is hard work. Mountaineers must eat food that contains a large amount of energy. Their food must also be easy to carry.

Energy is measured in units called kilojoules, or kJ for short. A bar of chocolate contains over 3,000 kilojoules of energy. A sandwich of the same size contains less than one-quarter of this energy. So mountaineers who get to the top carry chocolate!

This chart shows the energy needs of different people. Energy is measured in units called kilojoules, or kJ for short.

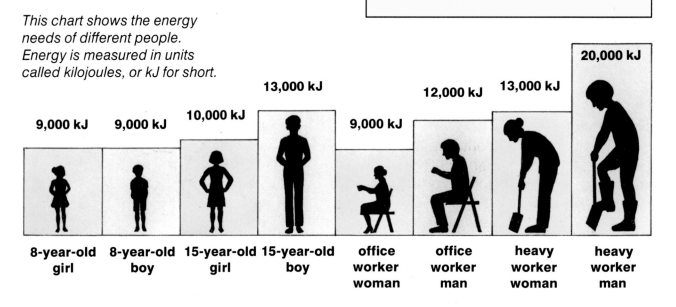

9,000 kJ	9,000 kJ	10,000 kJ	13,000 kJ	9,000 kJ	12,000 kJ	13,000 kJ	20,000 kJ
8-year-old girl	8-year-old boy	15-year-old girl	15-year-old boy	office worker woman	office worker man	heavy worker woman	heavy worker man

Different foods contain different amounts of energy.

baked beans 200 kJ	potatoes 340 kJ	lettuce 1 kJ	peanut butter 2,600 kJ	red meat 870 kJ

amount of energy in 100 grams (3½ ounces)

Atoms and molecules

Everything in the world is either a solid, a liquid, or a gas. All solids, liquids, and gases are made up from matter. Matter has mass and takes up space. You measure the mass of a substance by weighing it. All matter is made from tiny particles called atoms. The atoms in most substances are joined together in separate groups called molecules.

Pasta is a solid. It is firm and keeps its shape because the molecules in it are pressed together. Orange juice is a liquid. It is runny because the molecules slide easily past each other. You can pour a liquid from one container to another.

Gases include the smells that are given off when food is cooking. Gas molecules are completely free from each other. They spread out to fill the whole of the space that they are in.

Food contains very complicated molecules. You obtain energy from food when your body breaks these molecules into smaller pieces.

Look closely at some grains of salt. Each grain is shaped like a tiny box and is called a crystal. The arrangement of the atoms inside a crystal decides its shape.

Salt crystals contain two different kinds of separate atoms. The atoms are arranged in a regular pattern that is repeated over and over again. The pattern in each crystal is the same. Salt crystals can be different sizes, but they always have the same shape.

solid

gas

liquid

Toffee apples

Equipment

4 popsicle sticks
food scale
a measuring cup
a teaspoon
a heavy-based saucepan
a wooden board
wax paper or baking parchment

1 Wash and dry the apples. Push a stick into the core of each apple through the stem end.

2 Put the sugar in the saucepan. Add the water and the syrup to the pot.

3 Heat the pot over a very low heat. Do not stir the mixture. Move the pot around gently until the sugar has dissolved and no sugar crystals can be seen.

4 Ask an adult to help you bring the mixture to a boil. Boil it for 6 minutes. Be very careful as the mixture gets very hot and bubbles up in the pot.

5 Carefully transfer the hot pot onto a wooden board. Tilt the pot slightly. Hold an apple by its stick and dip it into the hot toffee. Make sure you do not touch the hot toffee with your fingers.

6 Lift up the apple and turn it around above the pot for a few seconds. This allows any extra toffee to drip off. You need to work fairly quickly as the toffee will begin to harden.

7 Place the toffee apple on the wax paper or baking parchment. Repeat with the other three apples. Leave the apples to cool and harden before eating.

What's in food?

There are many different kinds of food, but they are all made up from just seven main substances. These substances are carbohydrates, proteins, fats, water, vitamins, minerals, and fiber.

Carbohydrates and fats give us energy to move about and to do work. Rice, potatoes, and pasta contain large amounts of carbohydrate. Cream and margarine are mostly fat. Meat contains fat as well.

Protein from foods like meat, beans, and eggs helps your body to grow. It also helps to repair the worn-out parts of your body. Water dissolves substances and moves them around inside your body. Water makes up 95 percent of a tomato and 75 percent of an egg.

Vitamins and minerals keep you healthy. Many of them are found in fruit and vegetables. Fiber is found in vegetables and whole wheat flour. It helps to move food through your body.

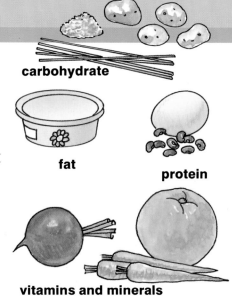

carbohydrate

fat

protein

vitamins and minerals

water

fiber

eggs:
weight 100 g
energy 610 kJ
protein 12.3 g
carbohydrate 0.4 g
fat 10.9 g

apple juice:
volume 100 ml
energy 186 kJ
protein 0.1 g
carbohydrate 11.5 g
fat 0 g

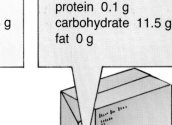

bar of chocolate:
weight 100 g
energy 2,085 kJ
protein 3.7 g
carbohydrate 56.7 g
fat 30.1 g

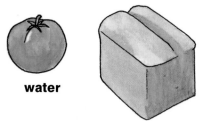

The labels on packaged food tell you what the food inside contains. They tell you how much carbohydrate, fat, protein, and fiber is found in a certain quantity of each food. This information is called nutritional information.

More and more products are carrying nutritional information on their packaging. So you can compare the amount of fats, for example, in different packaged foods by looking at their labels. Some packages also tell how much energy is contained in the food.

Cheese and tomato pizza

Ingredients

1 teaspoon dried yeast
1 teaspoon sugar
2½ fl oz warm water
5 oz whole wheat flour
salt and pepper

2 teaspoons vegetable oil
2 tablespoons tomato puree
2 tablespoons water
1 teaspoon dried basil
or mixed herbs
3½ oz mozarella cheese

Equipment

a teaspoon
a measuring cup
food scale
a large bowl
a wooden spoon
a tablespoon
a small bowl
a cheese grater
a pastry board
a baking tray
a rolling pin

1 Measure the warm water into the measuring cup, and add the yeast and sugar. Stir until the sugar has dissolved. Leave the cup in a warm place for 15 minutes until the mixture is frothy on top.

2 Put the flour into the large bowl. Add the salt and mix it in. Make a hollow in the center of the flour.

3 Add the oil into the middle of the hollow. Pour in the warm water mixture. Stir with a wooden spoon. With your hands, form the mixture into a lump of dough.

4 Sprinkle a little flour onto a work surface, and turn the dough out onto it. Knead the dough for 5 minutes. Add a little more flour if the dough is sticky.

5 Roll out the dough into a circle measuring 8 inches across. Sprinkle a light covering of flour over the baking tray and place the dough on it. Let it rise in a warm place for about 30 minutes.

6 Preheat the oven to 425°F. Grate the cheese. Put the tomato puree, water, salt, pepper, and herbs into the small bowl. Mix together well.

7 When the dough has risen, use the back of the tablespoon to spread the tomato mixture evenly over the dough. Sprinkle the grated cheese on top. Bake the pizza for 15–20 minutes. Carefully remove it from the oven, and serve hot or cold.

Food in your body

You need food to stay alive, active, and healthy. But what happens to your food after you swallow it? Food passes through your body in a coiled pipe called the alimentary canal. Inside your stomach and small intestine, special liquids called digestive juices are made. These juices break your food down into a soupy mixture of simple substances.

The lining of part of your small intestine is folded into tiny fingerlike shapes, called villi. The simple substances from your digested food are taken, or absorbed, into the bloodstream through the villi. Blood carries energy and nourishment to all parts of your body.

The large intestine absorbs water and minerals from the undigested part of your food. It leaves behind the solid waste matter. Fiber from vegetables, fruit, bran, and whole wheat flour is not digested. It helps food to move through the alimentary canal.

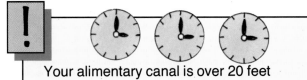

!

Your alimentary canal is over 20 feet long. Food takes up to 24 hours to pass through it. Food stays in your stomach for between 1 and 6 hours. It stays in your small intestine for 4 to 8 hours, and in your large intestine for 10 to 12 hours.

Inside the small intestine are over 5 million villi. Each one is about 1 millimeter long. The total surface area of all the villi is over 750 square feet, which is about half the area of a tennis court!

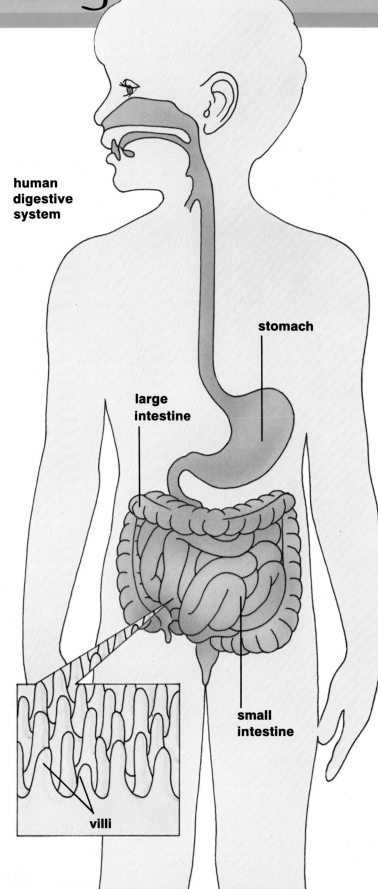

human digestive system

stomach

large intestine

small intestine

villi

Crunchy muesli

Ingredients

3oz rolled oats
3oz natural bran flakes
3oz wheat flakes
2oz dried apricots
2oz raisins
2oz shelled nuts, such
as hazelnuts, almonds,
Brazil nuts

Equipment

food scale
a large bowl
a cutting board
a knife
an airtight container, such as a
plastic box or a screw-top jar

1 Put the oats, the bran flakes, and the wheat flakes in the large bowl.

2 Chop the apricots into pieces and add them to the bowl. Add the raisins.

3 Chop the nuts into small pieces and add them to the bowl. Mix everything together with your hands. Serve the muesli with milk or yogurt. Keep any spare muesli in an airtight container.

What are proteins?

Meat, fish, milk, eggs, beans, and wheat are foods that are good sources of protein. Why do you need to eat proteins, and what happens to them inside your body?

Most of your body is made up from water and proteins. Different kinds of proteins help to make up your skin, muscles, and blood. During digestion, the proteins you eat are broken into simpler parts, called amino acids. These amino acids are then joined together again by special processes that provide the proteins to make up your body parts.

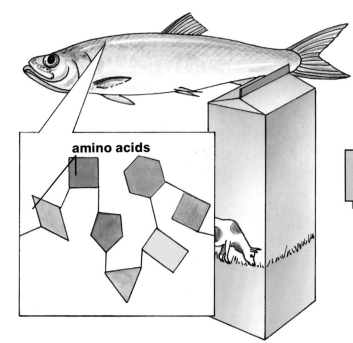

amino acids

This process is rather like breaking a house into piles of bricks, and then using the same bricks to build a new house with a different shape. So perhaps the hamburger you ate yesterday has helped your muscles to grow larger and has replaced some worn-out skin.

! The molecules that make up proteins are thousands of times bigger than the molecules that make up water. Each protein molecule is shaped like a long piece of spaghetti that is coiled into a special shape.

When you cook a piece of meat, it becomes tender. When you cook meringues, the beaten egg whites set hard and crispy. Heat causes the protein molecules in food to uncoil, and then to rearrange themselves in a different shape. This rearrangement of the protein alters the texture and appearance of the food.

Fruit meringue pudding

Ingredients

2 cups fruit, such as peaches, strawberries, kiwi fruit, raspberries

2 eggs

2 tablespoons superfine sugar

Equipment

an ovenproof dish
a tablespoon
a cutting board
a knife
2 small bowls
a large bowl
an electric mixer

1 Wash and halve the peaches. Take out the pits and slice the peaches. Peel and slice the kiwi fruit. Wash the strawberries and raspberries.

2 Arrange the fruit in the bottom of the ovenproof dish. Preheat the oven to 500°F.

3 Carefully separate one egg over a small bowl. Make sure that no yolk is left behind with the white. Put the white into the large bowl. Repeat with the second egg.

4 Beat the whites until they are stiff and no longer move about when you tilt the bowl.

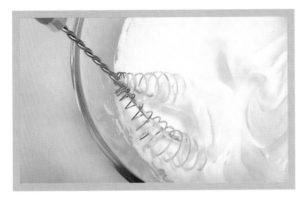

5 Add the sugar to the egg whites and beat again for 1 minute. The mixture should become thick and look shiny.

6 Spread the beaten egg white over the fruit. Make the egg white stand up in peaks by lifting it with the back of the spoon.

7 Carefully put the dish into the hot oven and bake for 5 minutes until the meringue is golden brown. Using oven mitts, remove the dish and serve immediately.

What are carbohydrates?

Energy to move about and to do work comes from the fats and the carbohydrates that you eat. Rice, potatoes, pasta, and wheat are all good sources of a common carbohydrate called starch. They all come from plants, which take in water and minerals from the soil as they grow. Plants also take in carbon dioxide gas from the air. During a process called photosynthesis, energy from sunlight joins these substances together. This makes a carbohydrate called glucose, which plants use for food.

Glucose is a simple type of sugar. Molecules of glucose are joined together in plants to make more complicated carbohydrates such as starch. The starch that you eat and digest is broken down inside your body into separate molecules of glucose. When you take in oxygen from the air you breathe, this glucose is changed back into carbon dioxide and water. This process is called respiration. At the same time, energy is released in your body.

Athletes use drinks or tablets that contain pure glucose. The glucose dissolves quickly into their bloodstream and gives them "instant energy." When you are resting, you need energy that is equal to about two teaspoons of glucose every hour. If you go swimming, you use five times this amount of energy.

If you eat more carbohydrate than you need, it will be stored in your body as fat. Many people eat too much carbohydrate, especially in the form of ordinary sugar.

energy in

oxygen out

oxygen in

carbohydrate

carbon dioxide

energy out

water in

water out

PHOTOSYNTHESIS

RESPIRATION

Homemade pasta

Ingredients

1 egg
3 oz semolina or strong plain flour, or a mixture of both
a pinch of salt
extra flour for rolling

Equipment

a bowl
a fork
a sieve
a large pastry board
a rolling pin
a knife
a plastic bag
a large pot
a colander

1 Break the egg into the bowl. Beat it with the fork until the white and yolk are thoroughly combined.

2 Sieve the semolina or flour into the bowl. Mix the flour and eggs together with the fork at first. Then press the mixture together with your hands to form a dough.

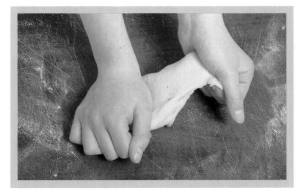

3 Sprinkle some flour onto the board and turn out the dough. Knead the dough firmly for 10 minutes until it is stretchy, but not sticky. Sprinkle on a little more flour if the dough is sticky.

4 Put the kneaded dough into the plastic bag. Leave it to rest for 30 minutes. Put the dough back on the board and start to roll it out as thinly as possible.

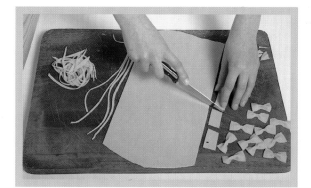

5 Keep turning the dough to prevent it from sticking to the board. Add a little more flour if needed. (Too much flour will dry out the pasta too quickly.)

6 Cut the pasta into thin noodles or bows. Leave it to dry out on the board for about 30 minutes. Ask an adult to help you bring a pot of water to a boil.

7 Carefully add the pasta to the boiling water and cook for 5 minutes. Remove from the heat and drain through a colander placed in the bottom of the sink. Serve with grated cheese or tomato sauce.

What are fats?

If you fry sausages, bacon, and eggs in a frying pan, you will have a meal that contains plenty of fat. This fat provides your body with twice as much energy as the same amount of carbohydrate. If you are very busy and active, you will use up all the fat that you eat. But if you live a sedentary and inactive life, the fat will be stored under your skin. This layer of fat helps to keep you warm, but it also makes your body heavier and fatter.

In some countries, people use avocados instead of butter. The creamy inside part of an avocado is made up from about 20 percent fat. It is good to spread on bread when butter or margarine is not available. The avocado is sometimes called "poor person's butter."

Many foods contain "hidden" fat. Ice cream contains more than 10 percent fat, cookies over 20 percent, and chocolate is about 50 percent fat. People who want to lose weight try to avoid eating these foods.

energy from carbohydrate

energy from fat

A person can cycle three times further after eating five chocolate cookies (100 grams) than after eating three slices of whole wheat bread (100 grams).

Oils are fats, too, but they are usually in a liquid form. Most of the oils that we eat come from plants such as olive trees and sunflowers. Most of the solid fats that we eat come from animals. Many doctors believe that it is healthier to eat oils from plants rather than fats from animals.

Oils and solid fats do not dissolve when they are mixed with water. Instead, they form droplets in the water. Milk is made up from tiny particles of fat in water. Solid cheese is made by removing the water from milk, leaving behind the solid fat.

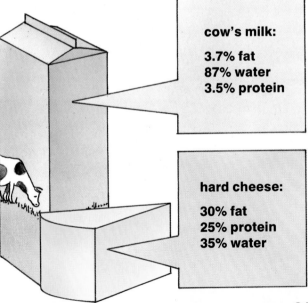

cow's milk:

3.7% fat
87% water
3.5% protein

hard cheese:

30% fat
25% protein
35% water

Avocado dip

Ingredients
1 ripe avocado
half of a small lemon
1 tablespoon mayonnaise
salt and pepper

Equipment

a cutting board
a knife
a small bowl
a lemon squeezer
2 tablespoons
a fork

1 Cut the avocado in half and remove the pit. If this is difficult, ask an adult to help you. Use a spoon to scoop out the flesh, and put it in the bowl.

2 Squeeze out the juice from the lemon. Add the juice to the bowl, making sure you leave the pits behind in the squeezer.

3 Add the mayonnaise and some salt and pepper to the bowl. Mash together the ingredients with a fork until they are well combined. Serve the avocado dip with a selection of raw vegetables.

Vitamins and minerals?

When you cook carrots in boiling water, they become soft and tender. Although cooked carrots are easier to eat than raw ones, they are less nutritious. Like most plants, carrots contain tiny amounts of a substance called carotene. Your body changes carotene into another substance, called vitamin A. Without vitamin A, your eyes do not work properly and your skin becomes dry and scaly. Heat, for example from boiling water, or strong light destroys this carotene.

! Over 200 years ago, many sailors on long sea voyages died from a disease called scurvy. In 1768, an Englishman called Captain James Cook began a three-year journey sailing around the South Seas. His crew set a record for those days because only one sailor died out of 118. This was because Captain Cook added lemon juice to the water drunk by the sailors. Lemons contain vitamin C, and we now know that a lack of vitamin C causes scurvy.

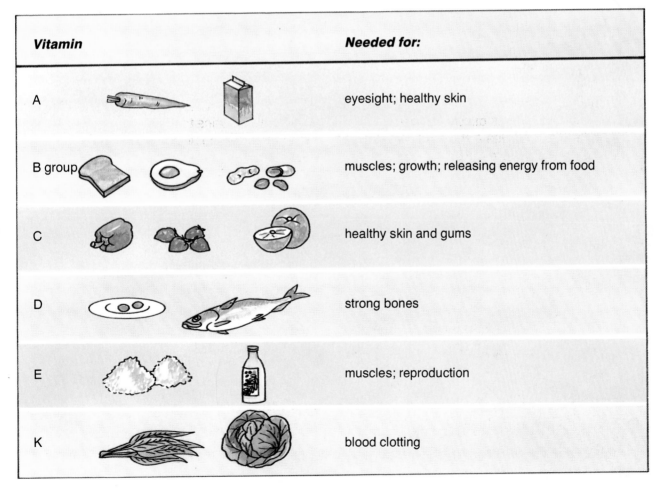

Vitamin		Needed for:
A		eyesight; healthy skin
B group		muscles; growth; releasing energy from food
C		healthy skin and gums
D		strong bones
E		muscles; reproduction
K		blood clotting

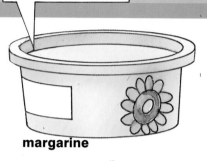

vitamins A, D, E

margarine

Vitamin C is found in certain fruits, such as oranges, lemons, grapefruits, and kiwi fruit, and in vegetables such as cabbage and broccoli. Another name for vitamin C is ascorbic acid. It helps your skin and gums to stay healthy.

There are 12 other main vitamins that your body needs in order to stay healthy. You cannot make most of these vitamins inside your body, so you must eat foods that contain them. The amounts of these vitamins that you need are very small – a few thousandths of a gram each day. The vitamins are not broken down by digestion but pass directly into your bloodstream.

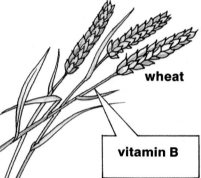

wheat

vitamin B

Fruit salad

Ingredients
2 oranges
2 kiwi fruit
3 oz purple grapes

Equipment

paper towels
a cutting board
a knife
a serving plate

1 Rinse the oranges and kiwi fruit under cold water, then dry them with the paper towels. Wash the grapes and leave them to drain on a piece of paper towel.

2 Cut off both ends of each orange. Remove the peel and the white pith by cutting down the orange towards the board. Slice the orange into circles.

vitamins A, C, E

vitamins A, B, D, E, K

eggs

tomatoes

vitamins A, B

peas and beans

vitamins A, B, C, E, K

vitamins A, B, D, E, K

liver

green vegetables

3 Prepare the kiwi fruit in the same way as the orange. Cut the grapes in half. Remove any seeds with the tip of the knife.

4 Arrange the prepared fruit on the serving plate. Serve the fruit salad as soon as possible.

Everybody drinks milk as a baby at the beginning of their life. Milk contains a substance called calcium, which helps you to grow strong bones and teeth.

Calcium is a kind of mineral. It consists of a simple atom that is found in the ground. Calcium is taken up from the ground by plants, such as grass and corn. Animals that make milk eat these plants. In this way, the calcium passes from the ground to the plant, and then to the animal and the milk, and finally to you.

You may use salt to bring out the flavor in your food. Salt contains a mineral called sodium. The nerves that carry messages around your body need sodium. Animals contain more sodium than plants. So you need to add more salt when cooking vegetables than you do when cooking meat. Spinach and liver contain another mineral called iron. A regular supply of iron helps your body to make new supplies of blood.

You need to take in about 12 different minerals to stay healthy. If you weigh 66 lb, then your body contains about 5 tablespoons of calcium, 1 tablespoon of sodium, and the same amount of iron as in a large nail.

Salt was a very valuable substance 2,000 years ago. Roman soldiers were paid a sum of money, called a *salarium*, to buy their salt. From this name comes the modern word "salary."

Mineral	Source			Role in
calcium	milk, beans			bones, teeth
phosphorus	milk, eggs			bones, teeth, energy release
sodium	table salt			body fluids, nerve function
potassium	fruit juices			body fluids, nerve function
chlorine	table salt			stomach digestive juices
magnesium	fruit juice			bones, nerve function
iron	liver, beans			blood
sulfur	meat, milk, eggs			making proteins
iodine	sea salt, fish			thyroid gland (controls the metabolism of your body)

Healthy eating

Doughnuts, potato chips, and candy taste good to eat. Yet what would happen if you ate only these foods and nothing else? Many processed foods like these contain a lot of added salt, sugary carbohydrate, and fat. You would not be taking in enough protein, fiber, vitamins, or minerals. You would not be eating a healthy, balanced diet. You would suffer from malnutrition, which is the result of eating too little or the wrong kinds of food.

Many people are overweight because they eat too much food. Others are not healthy because the food they eat does not contain enough vitamins and minerals, or because it contains too much fat and not enough starchy carbohydrate.

Foods like chicken, fish, vegetables, beans, and whole wheat bread are much better for your body. If you eat the right amounts of these foods, you will be eating a healthy, balanced diet.

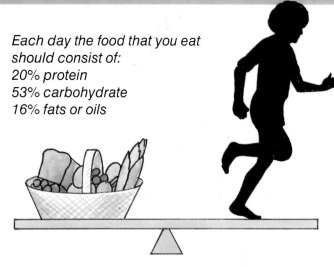

Each day the food that you eat should consist of:
20% protein
53% carbohydrate
16% fats or oils

The energy in the food that you eat must balance the work that you do.

Over one-half of a balanced diet should consist of carbohydrate. One-fifth should be protein, and about one-sixth should be fats or oils. You need only tiny amounts of most of the different vitamins and minerals. Just a few milligrams, which is less than a tiny pinch of flour, are enough.

Young people who are growing need more protein than adults. It is better to obtain your protein from fish and beans, for example, than from sausages or bacon, which contain a lot of animal fat.

Eat more of these foods

Eat less of these foods

Chinese steamed vegetables

Ingredients

4 scallions
2 oz snow pea pods or green beans
3 oz baby corn
1 small red pepper
2 small zucchini
1 tablespoon sesame seeds
1 tablespoon soy sauce
1 tablespoon salad oil

Equipment

a cutting board
a knife
a saucepan with a steamer
 and lid
a small bowl
a tablespoon
a fork
a serving dish

1 Half-fill the saucepan with water. Ask an adult to help you bring it to a boil. Wash all the vegetables.

2 Cut off the bulbs of the scallions, and remove the outer leaves. Cut the onions into short lengths. Trim the ends off the snow peas or green beans. Cut the beans in half.

3 Remove the core and seeds from the pepper. Slice the pepper into long pieces. Slice the zucchini into circles, and throw away the stalk end. Cut the corn cobs into short lengths.

4 Place the vegetables in the steamer. Ask an adult to help you put the steamer over the pot of boiling water. Put on the lid and steam the vegetables for about 5 minutes.

5 While the vegetables are cooking, put the sesame seeds, soy sauce, and oil in the bowl. Whisk together with a fork.

6 After 5 minutes the vegetables will be cooked but still crunchy. Ask an adult to remove the steamer from the pot. Transfer the vegetables to the serving dish.

7 Pour the sesame seed mixture over the vegetables and serve at once. The vegetables are delicious with homemade pasta (see pages 19–20).

Further things to do

Push a peanut onto the end of a sewing needle. Ask an adult to hold the peanut over a flame until it catches fire. The peanut will burn by itself, giving out large amounts of heat energy. When you eat a peanut it gives out the same amount of energy, but more slowly.

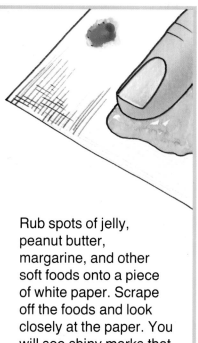

Pour water into a glass jar to a depth of ¾ inches. Ask an adult to add two drops of brown iodine solution to the jar. Add a pinch of some powdered starch, such as cornstarch, and stir. The starch turns a blue-black color. Try this test with different foods, such as flour, pudding powder, and dried milk. Find out which ones contain the carbohydrate starch.

Rub spots of jelly, peanut butter, margarine, and other soft foods onto a piece of white paper. Scrape off the foods and look closely at the paper. You will see shiny marks that allow light to pass through. These marks are made by foods that contain fats or oils.

Make a note of all the different foods you eat in a day, and of the amount of each food that you eat. Use the nutritional information on food packages to figure out how much energy you have taken in. You need about 9,000 kilojoules of energy each day. Is your diet balanced for energy? Does the energy you take in equal the energy you give out?

Add two teaspoons of lemon juice to a quarter of a glass of milk. Stir the mixture and leave it for 30 minutes. The lemon juice makes the fat and protein particles in the milk break down and stick together. They separate from the water in the milk and sink to the bottom of the glass.

Glossary

alimentary canal
A long tube inside your body that digests food and takes in nourishment from it

amino acid
One of 20 different types of molecules that are found in proteins

atom
The smallest part of any substance. There are about 100 different kinds of atom.

balanced diet
A selection of foods that contain the right daily amounts of carbohydrate, fats and oils, protein, vitamins, minerals, fiber, and water

bloodstream
The flow of blood which carries the nourishment from your food around your body

carbohydrate
A food substance that is used as a source of energy. Sugar and starch are carbohydrates.

crystal
A small piece of solid with straight sides. Salt and sugar are made up from crystals.

digestion
A process inside your body that breaks food down into smaller pieces so that it can be used

digestive juice
A liquid which is made in the stomach and intestine to break down food

energy
Energy makes things "do work." You need energy from food to move about and to do things.

fat
A food substance that is used as a source of energy. Layers of fat keep you warm.

fiber
A substance in food that is not affected by digestion. It helps to move food through your body.

glucose
A kind of sugar that is made by digesting starch

intestine
A long tube inside your body in which food is digested, then passes into the bloodstream

kilojoule
A unit for measuring energy. One kilojoule (kJ for short) will boil half a teaspoon of water.

mass
A measurement that shows how much matter is in something. The unit of mass is the pound.

matter
Everything is made from matter. It has mass or weight and takes up space.

mineral
A food substance that is made up from one type of atom only. Minerals keep us healthy.

molecule
A tiny part that makes up most substances. All the molecules in a substance are the same. Each molecule contains two or more atoms.

oil
A fat that is usually a liquid

protein
A food substance that you use for growth and to repair parts of your body

starch
A carbohydrate which is found in rice, flour, and potatoes

stomach
The part of the alimentary canal that carries out the first stage of food digestion

sugar
A simple carbohydrate, such as glucose or ordinary sugar

vitamin
A substance that must be in your food in order for you to be healthy

Index